TU'I TONGA

…a commentary on names, events and
early history of Tonga's ancient Kings…

SEMISI PONE

CONTENTS

List of Tu'i Tonga

Introduction................1
The Tu'i Tonga Line.........2

List of Tu'i Tonga and associated events

1. 'Aho'eitu.........................5
2. Lolofakangalo..................9
3. Fanga'one'one.................10
4. Lihau......................13
5. Kofutu.........................14
6. Kaloa.............................15
7. Ma'uhau...........................17
8. 'Apuanea.............................19
9. 'Afulunga....................20
10. Momo.......................22
11. Tu'itatui......................25
12. Talatama........................27
13. Tu'itonganui koe Tamatou.........31
14. Talaiha'apepe....................33
15. Talakaifaiki........................35
16. Talafapite.......................37
17. Ma'akatoe......................38

18. Puipuifatu I...............39
19. Havea I........................40
20. Tatafu'eikimeimu'a...........42
21. Lomi'aetupu'a.................44
22. Havea II...................45
23. Takalaua......................46
24. Kau'ulufonua I............49
25. Vakafuhu......................53
26. Puipuifatu II.......................54
27. Kau'ulufonua II.................55
28. Tapu'osi I.....................56
29. 'Uluakimata I..................58
30. Fatafehi.........................61
31. Tapu'osi II/Kau'ulufonua III....63
32. 'Uluakimata II....................65
33. Tu'ipulotu I ('ilangitu'ofefafa)...68
34. Fakana'ana'a.....................71
35. Tu'ipulotu II ('ilangitu'oteau)....74
36. Paulaho...........................79
37. Ma'ulupekotofa..............83
38. Fuanunu'iava..................85
39. Laufilitonga..................88

Important titles of the Tu'i Tonga
        Era and the office holders.........96

Why did the Tu'i Tonga
Dynasty end?..........................101

Stories associated with the Tu'i
Tonga...............................104

Abbreviations..................…..128

References cited.................…......130

About the author..................….....135

List of figures

Figure 1........................127

Introduction

This book is a commentary and added opinion of the author using various sources published in the Tongan and English languages. The idea is to provide information for our young people who wish to know something about ancient Tongan kings. The history, meaning of names, immediate royal families and their wives and children.The author adds comments and oral history to written references listed in the further reading list with the aim of encouraging critical thought on the available history and clarifying some points.

The book is also intended as a student resource for the planned University of Polynesia (universityofpolynesia.com) currently under public consultation. Much of this information will be unavailable to young Tongans and Polynesian students of the university who cannot read Tongan publications hence this publication will be a valuable tool for students.

The Tu'i Tonga[1] Line

 The Tu'i Tonga is a line of Tongan kings, which originated from Tangaroa probably in the fifth century[13]. 'Aho'eitu son of Tangaroa was the first king. In the 1400s the 23rd Tu'i Tonga, Takalaua, established the Tu'i Ha'a Takalaua[27] and withdrew from political power. In around 1600, the 6th Tu'i Ha'a Takalaua, Mo'ungatonga installed his son Ngata as the Tu'i Kanokupolu[28] which quickly rose to power supported by Ngata's Samoan relatives. His mother Tohu'ia came from the island of 'Upolu in Samoa hence the name 'Kakano 'o 'Upolu' or 'flesh of 'Upolu'. It can also mean 'originate from 'Upolu'. The name is shortened to Kanokupolu[17].

Traditionally Tu'i Tonga names include 39 holders of the title, but there is an alternative list with 48 names by Rev

Shirley Baker. Tevita Fale also offers a list of 54. See Figure 1.

This book will deal exclusively with the Tu'i Tonga and information about each king, commentary on the Tu'i Ha'a Takalaua and Tu'i Kanokupolu will follow at a later date.

LIST OF TU'I TONGA AND EVENTS

This list of Tu'i Tonga is according to the 'Catholic records' as proposed in the Tu'i Tonga diagram in Figure 1. Although there are variations in the names of some Tu'i Tonga in the records I have not made an attempt to correct them according to the sources used in this book.

It is the author's view that the variations in the names on the record does bring in new interpretations and meaning to each record. Future researchers can draw their own conclusions from their research and interpretations.

For example, the name of the 17th Tu'i Tonga used in this book and sources is Ma'akatoe but on the list in Figure 1, it is Ma'akatoa which has a totally different meaning (all clean cf TT17 explanations).

4

Tu'i Tonga 1

'Aho'eitu

The name 'Aho'eitu means 'day of the Gods'. Youngest son of Tangaroa, the divine father, around 900 AD (cf 400 AD[13]), resided first in Popua and then other places of the Hahake district, like Toloa near Fua'amotu. Dr Siaosi 'Ilaiu[13] proposed a date of nearer 400 AD (CE) for the establishment of the first Tu'i Tonga (TT), 'Aho'eitu. That may be consistent with the lists of 48 or even 54 kings as proposed by others in Figure 1.

Mahina[14] wrote, *'Aho'eitu was possibly of Samoan-Niuan extraction; peak of first probable eastern Polynesian influences, via hegemony and counter-hegemony of two regional cultures, Pulotu and Langi, over Maama or Lolofonua, connected with rise of three principal deities; antagonised*

*Pulotu and Langi, then founded Tu'i
Tonga dynasty on Maama, or Tonga.*

In my book[6], I propose that Tangaroa
came from Eastern Polynesia possibly a
descendant of white gods from Persia
migrating through South America as
proposed by Thor Heyerdahl and others[15].

According to Tongan Oral History[10], the
children of Tangaloa 'Eitumatupu'a were;

1. Talafale
2. Tu'iloloko
3. Maliepo
4. Tu'ifolaha
5. Matakehe
who had the same mother.
6. 'Aho'eitu.
whose mother is Va'epopua 'Ilaheva.

There is a suggestion that Va'epopua
'Ilaheva was the daughter of the Tu'i
Ha'amea[10].

Talafale became the Tu'i Faleua ancestor of
the Lord Tu'i Pelehake line. It is worth
mentioning that many of the ancient lines
were replaced by subsequent monarchs. For

example, the current Lord Tu'i Pelehake is the grandson of King Taufa'ahau Tupou IV's brother Fatafehi (Tu'ipelehake). In most instances the ancient line may have ended with a barren title holder or in some cases the title was bestowed by the king on another family, disregarding the claims of the original title holders[17]. One example is the title Ma'atu which King Taufa'ahau Tupou IV bestowed on his third child 'Alaivahamama'o. Tongan supporters of the king claim that the king owns all the titles and the estates and has the divine and traditional right to install anyone to any title or estate[17].

Tu'iloloko, Maliepo, Tu'ifolaha and Matakehe became the Falefa who were traditional protectors of the Tu'i Tonga[10].

Tu'iloloko gave rise to two titles Tu'uhokokilangi and Malupo (not Lord Malupo). Maliepo gave rise to the title Lauaki which is one of the King's talking Chiefs during the Royal Kava Ceremony (the other being Motu'apuaka)[17] and also Royal Undertaker. This title is given the estate of Talafo'ou. The Tu'i Folaha gave rise to the titles 'Aholangamakahiva and Mailau[10].

Matakehe's descendants are not found in the records. He may have passed away or his line died out without any present day descendants[17]. Again, it is the king's prerogative to install or abolish titles[17] but may also depend on lobbying by the families to have their title 'revived'. In many cases families view titles as a burden and huge cost for the family who have to meet traditional obligations to the king and 'fonua' meaning relatives and the Tongan public[17]. The family may choose to ignore or even support abolishing the title, especially if its one of the low ranked ones with no estate[17].

Tu'i Tonga 2

Lolofakangalo

The name means 'scented oil of slow disappearance'[14] or 'oil of forgetfulness'. It could also mean a lubricant for sexual activity[17].

Mahina adds, possibly symbolic of Pulotu and Langi being squeezed out of social scene; little is known about this Tu'i Tonga, except his name[14].

Tu'i Tonga 3

Fanga'one'one

The name means 'beach of sand' as opposed to Fangamakamaka[17] or 'beach of stones'. It is possible that this Tu'i Tonga was born near a beach at Popua as in ancient times the lagoon waters was clear, not muddy like today, and beaches were sandy as observed by Mary Lawry[12] at Mu'a in 1822.

Fale[18] proposes that Fanga'one'one was the Tu'i Tonga's resident at Popua near the original spot where Tangaloa arrived from the sky and saw the mortal woman Va'epopua 'Ilaheva.

Fale had also proposed the list of 54 names of Kings for the Tu'i Tonga Dynasty as seen in Figure I.

In most ancient history of many countries, their ancestor arriving from the sky is a common occurrence. Even in the Bible in Genesis 6 for example[17];

Genesis 6:1-2

> *And it came to pass, when men began to multiply on the face of the earth, and daughters were born unto them, That the sons of God saw the daughters of men that they were fair; and they took them wives of all which they chose.*

This verse from the Christian Bible suggest that the 'sons of God' came down from the sky and took mortal women as their wives. The same idea in the Tangaloa and Va'epopua story where Tangaloa came down from the sky climbing down a toa (*Casuarina equisetifolia*) tree[17].

Mahina writes, 'it (Fanga'one'one) may be representative of shoreline movement of early the Tu'i Tonga (TT) from Popua

through Folaha to Pelehake. This TT is
only known by his name[14].'

Tu'i Tonga 4

Lihau

The name means 'throwing of the conqueror'. It could have been a period of popular wrestling where the name originate from. Wrestling was one of the ancient Tongan sports. Little is known about Lihau; his name is of Niuan-'Uvean extraction[14].

The name could also be a reference to the Tongan calendar where the months of Lihamu'a and Lihamui represent the period from mid-November to mid-January. It is a period of relative calm and warm weather. The words 'Liha' and 'u' meaning 'period of calm weather'. The word u is usually referred to a calm refuge like in a port for canoes, in ancient times, hence 'taulanga u' or 'port of calm refuge'[17].

Tu'i Tonga 5

Kofutu

The name Kofutu means 'tired of waiting'[17]or 'waiting for a long time' but could also mean 'from Futu' or 'it is Futu' a place name. The word is used in the Free Wesleyan Church Hymn, for example, to describe a person tired of waiting *'Kofutu 'eku mo'utalia'*[17].

Futu is also a name of a tree (*Barringtonia speciosa).* A name given in Samoa and Tonga to a handsome littoral tree having 4 cornered pyramidal fruit, the outer portion of which is used by the natives as a fish-intoxicant[16].

Elongated-(time-period); little is known of Kofutu, except his name being of Niuan-'Uvean origin[14].

Tu'i Tonga 6

Kaloa

The name Kaloa means to 'duck and weave'[14] as in boxing, coming from the root word 'kalo', to move one's head to avoid a punch or object thrown at the head. Boxing was also an ancient Tongan sport. This period could have been a 'boxing era'. In war time, one of the ancient weapons of choice was the 'throwing club', but could also be used to describe ducking or avoiding a spear or arrows aimed at the head[17].

In Tongan history, it could also mean escaping an enemy or a threat[14].

Loa is also a tree with fruits used for face painting as in times of war or preparations for a dance ceremony. The expression kaloa maybe a reference to face painting[17].

'Escape, especially from difficult situations, moving head sideways, little is known of him; his name being of Niuan-'Uvean extraction[14].

Tu'i Tonga 7

Ma'uhau

The name Ma'uhau means 'provider of the champion/conquerer'. In ancient times the King was referred to as the 'Hau' or champion/conquerer. I had proposed in my book[6] that it could have originated from Hauaiki, or variation of Hou'eiki, in Eastern Polynesia, referring to the origin of Tangaroa. Hawaiki is the ancient name of the island of Raiatea near Tahiti in present day French Polynesia, the possible origin of the great fleet that came to New Zealand in 1350 AD (CE). Most general literature mention Maori trace their origin to the Great Fleet[17].

I had also suggested in my book[6] that the Great Fleet may have been the movement of the 'white gods' from Polynesia to Aotearoa. Maori refer to the 'white gods' as Patupaiarehe.

Receiver of power/tribute; connected with Lavengatonga Village, or 'Receiving -all-of-to n g a/T o n g a' - village, suggesting the early period to be one of nation building[14].

Tu'i Tonga 8

'Apuanea

Little is known of this Tu'i Tonga, except his name is Niuan-'Uvean in origin[14].

I should mention that there was a Tongan fort build in the island of 'Uvea probably in the 15th century known as Kolonui. The ruins can still be seen today[1]. There was a time that the early Tu'i Tonga (TT 4-9) may have resided or spent time at 'Uvea hence their 'Uvea/Samoan names[17].

Tu'i Tonga 9

'Afulunga

'Afulunga comes from the words *'afu* meaning 'hot and humid' and *lunga* meaning 'up' in Samoan[14]. It is also used as *'alunga*. Lunga is spelled *'olunga* in Tongan. *'Alunga* in Samoan often refers to the attic of the traditional fale where kava ('ava) and other valuable possessions are stored in ancient times[17].

Hot-up-top; possibly referring to warmer north; little is known about him, except his name is of Niuan-'Uvean extraction[14].

The children of 'Afulunga were Momo and Ngongokilitoto. There is no mention of the mother of Momo but Ngongokilitoto's mother was Kalikiva'e. There is a story about her name which means 'wooden pillow with foot' (kali or wooden pillow and va'e meaning foot), that she used to be carried around in a royal bearer or fata and she used to rest her feet on the bearer's heads[10].

Tu'i Tonga 10

Momo

Momo means fragments, usually of food (perhaps of traditions of early times); second wave of possible eastern Polynesian influences; represented final stages of nation building; formalised kava; laid down foundation for TT empire; married Nua, daughter of probable foreign figure, Lo'au, possibly an eastern Polynesian of Samoan descent[14].

The influence of Lo'au, the Tu'i Ha'amea, and his people from Eastern Polynesia was the catalyst for Tongan expansion and formation of the Tongan Maritime Empire. Queen Nua, daughter of Lo'au, that married Momo was probably the reason as the Eastern Polynesians may have out numbered all other islands and provides for the 'colonial' armies of the Tu'i Tonga[6]. The royal court in Heketā, where the Ha'amonga trillithon and Makafakinanga can be found, is near present day village of Niutōua[6].

The children of Momo[10] were;

1. Latutama who became the first Tu'i Tonga Fefine (female Tu'i Tonga) TTF1*
2. Tu'itatui TT11
3. Lelesi

* - It should be mentioned that when the oldest child of the Tu'i Tonga is a female, she is normally installed as a Tu'i Tonga Fefine or Female Tu'i Tonga and the oldest brother becomes the male Tu'i Tonga[17].

Momo left Lelesi in Tutu'ila (now American Samoa), in one of his voyages, and brought the son of Lautalakikite with him to become his talking chief, Leha'uli[10]. This was an account by a previous Leha'uli (Sione Ikapuna'imoana of Pelehake). Lelesi is suggested to be the origin of the Lelesi clan in Samoa[10].

In the story of Nua, Leha'uli was the talking chief sent by Momo to Lo'au requesting Nua's hand in marriage. The Leha'uli brought from Samoa was probably given the title after the previous Leha'uli passed away[17].

Nua had already had a child with the younger brother of Momo, Ngongokilitoto, named Fasi'apule, by the time Momo requested marriage. Fasi'apule was later installed by Momo to the title Tamale[17]. Tamale is a title still installed in the village of Niutoua to this day.

The alternative view (cf Eastern Polynesia origin of Lo'au[6]) would be that the son of Lautalakikite, who was the first Leha'uli[10], was brought by Momo from Tutu'ila to act as his talking chief because Lo'au was of mixed ancestry with Samoan/Eastern Polynesian listed by some scholars[14]. In that case, Leha'uli was brought to Tonga before Momo married Nua and not after[17]. The idea being, that Leha'uli would have a favorable rapport with Lo'au as they have common Samoan ancestry[17]. It suggests that Momo was totally besotted with Nua and had pulled out all the stops to win her hand in marriage[17].

Tu'i Tonga 11

Tu'itatui

Son of Momo and Nua around 1100 AD, the name means 'King hit knee', this king was a very tall man and probably had knee problems due to his weight[17]. Legend tells of his Makafakinanga or stone of rest, near the Ha'amonga trillithon, where the impression of his back and head while sitting down is about 6 feet high from ground to the top of his head. He would strike out with his war club at the knee of anyone coming close. Assassination of kings and chiefs was rife during those ancient times[17].

There is a story that the Makafakinanga was the head of the 'meeting circle' or where the king sits to greet visitors or chair important meetings[17].

Tu'itatui extended the royal court, built the Haʻamonga; re-established the Fale Fā (*house of four*), royal counselors and guardians; his cunning stepbrother Fasiʻapule became a governor[14].

Tu'i-tā-tui, means 'king-hit-knee', son of Momo and Nua; symbolic of his ability to put people on their knees; peak of second alleged wave of eastern Polynesian influences; major social reforms: reshuffled Falefa; developed Lo'au-Tu'itātui land tenure system; began regional imperial expansion by conquest[14].

The children of Tu'itatui [10]were;

1. Fatefehi TTF2
2. Talatama TT12
3. Talaiha'apepe TT14

It is suggested that the mother was Tu'itatui's own sister Latutama TTF1.

Tu'i Tonga 12

Talatama

The name means 'to tell'or 'to inform' a history or biography of a person usually a son or daughter. The story of the children of Tu'itatui and grandchildren of Momo and Nua is one of the most famous in Tongan history, just like the stories of Lo'au and Nua[17].

Talatama and Talaiha'apepe were getting constant complains from Fatafehi, their sister, of the noise of the surf at Heketā. They finally decided to move to a quieter place near the lagoon at Mu'a. Heketā was referred to as the 'Utulongoa'a (noisy beach), 'utu is a name for the rocky cliff facing the sea waves[17]. Longoa'a means noisy. The new royal place at Mu'a, near the lagoon, was quiet and was called the Fangalongonoa or 'quiet bay/beach'[17].

Here's an excerpt of the story[1].

Talatama is named as the oldest son of Tuʻitātui and succeeded him as the 12th Tuʻi Tonga somewhere in the middle of the 12th century AD.

They lived at Heketā, along the northcoast of Tongatapu, with its rocky shore. Launching and landing canoes was difficult and the surf of the sea was always noisy. The nearby village of Kolonga, nowadays is nicknamed ʻUtulongoaʻa

(noisy coast), because that was what Talatama's sister Fatafehi said.

Either to please her or just to find a better harbour for themselves Talatama and his younger brother Talaihaʻapepe decided to move the royal court to Muʻa (meaning: first, because as the new capital, the village would be the first to receive honours). Indeed, the coast there was sandy and muddy, safe for the boats, the big royal canoes, named ʻĀkiheuho and Tongafuesia, and it was quiet. The place was named Fangalongonoa (silent shore).

Since that time, up to the last Tu'i Tonga, Laufilitonga, the dynasty has always remained in Mu'a.

When Talatama died he had no sons. Talaiha'apepe seemed to be the most straightforward one to succeed him, but he himself saw it as a bad omen to break the tradition from father to son. Now when Talaiha'apepe had been a boy (some say he was still a boy at that time) he had a doll, made of tou wood, called Tamatou. This doll was declared the son of Talatama and installed with all the pomp and splendour of a Tu'i Tonga, even a queen was assigned to him, and he was named Tu'i-Tonga-nui-(ko-e)-tama-tou (Great Tonga king (that is) tou person).[1]

Three years later Talaiha'apepe declared that the king, Tamatou, had died and would be buried in a vault, while his wife was supposed to have been pregnant and born a son. This son, Talatama's grandson, would succeed as the 14th Tu'i Tonga. Needless to say that this was Talaiha'apepe himself.

There is also another story that the appointment of a 'piece of wood' to be king would fool assassins as a 'piece of wood' cannot be killed[17]. Note also the use of the word 'nui' in the title of the king, this word is of Eastern Polynesian origin and not normally used in Tonga[17].

Talatama means telling/traditions- of a child, son of Tu'itatui; possible reference to Tu'itatui's reforms; operated with Talaiha'apepe TT imperial fleet, led by two famous kalia , 'Akiheuho and Tongafuesia; probable last TT at Heketā, Niutoua[14].

Tu'i Tonga 13

Tu'i Tonga Nui koe Tamatou

Tuʻitonganui nui ko e Tamatou – said to have been a block of wood, standing in as child of Talatama and father of Talaihaʻapepe to keep the dynasty pure.

There is also another story suggesting that it was a ploy to fool would be assassins, because no one can kill a piece of wood…and because he is the son of the block of wood, cannot be assassinated. Similar to the problem of Tu'itatui, his children may have also faced threats[17].

Tu'i-tonga/Tonga-nui-koe-Tamatou, means Tu'i Tonga of greatness. The child of Tou tree, a wooden king made of tou wood; nui and tou, Tahitian in outlook, symbolic fragments of traditions from Eastern Polynesia; symbolic of possible Talatama and Talaiha'apepe title dispute;

reportedly buried in Langi Tamatou at
Makaunga/Niutao between Heketā in
Niutoua and Lapaha in Mu'a[14].

Tu'i Tonga 14

Talaiha'apepe

Talaiha'apepe is the real brother of Talatama and supposed grandson through the woodblock.

Talaiha'apepe/Ha'apepe, means telling of traditions at Ha'apepe/Ha'apepe (or Ha'apepa, one of major districts in Tahiti Nui) or Lineage of h a 'a p e p e /H a 'a p e p e /Ha'apepa); possible reference to some Tahitian body of ruling traditions; founded Lapaha, last and permanent TT imperial centre[14].

The children of Talaiha'apepe was;

1. Talakaifaiki TT 15

This king was also known as Talakaifaikifolaha[10]. According to Fale[18] the Tu'i Tonga had resided at Folaha and possibly at this time of Talakaifaikifolaha hence his name 'Talakaifaiki from folaha'[17].

Note the Eastern Polynesia influence possibly through Lo'au, Nua and their relatives[17].

Tu'i Tonga 15

Talakaifaiki

Talakaifaiki ruled around 1250 AD, start of the decline of the Tongan maritime empire, lost Samoa due to his cruelty to the Samoans prompting establishment of the Mālietoa title[14].

Talakaifaiki, means telling/traditions of eating/food done to; possibly symbolic of formal extraction of socio-economic wealth from periphery to centre; extended imperial expansion by conquest probably throughout Samoa; cruel subjugation of Samoa, which Samoans fiercely rebelled; driven out Talakaifaiki in series of wars; imperial expansion by conquest changed, possibly through treaty, to conquest-alliance formation[14].

The children of Talakaifaiki[10] were;

1. Talafapite TT16
2. Kakapu
3. Hahau

Kakapu and Hahau were twins whose
mother was Manuosoisinga from Samoa.
The son of Kakapu became Takapu 1 and
the son of Hahau became Hauta'ulu 1. They
had a sister who had a son to Lauaki
descendant of Maliepo of the Falefa (older
brother of 'Aho'eitu). The baby was named
Lauaki and he became the ancestor to the
Lauaki of today who is the Royal
Undertaker and Head of the Ha'a Tufunga[10].

Tu'i Tonga 16

Talafapite

Talafāpite means telling of traditions , body of traditions of Fapite, place or probably representative of some person; married and resided in Samoa[14].

The children of Talafapite was;

1. Ma'akatoe TT17

Tu'i Tonga 17

Ma'akatoe

Tu'i Tonga Ma'akatoe means 'Tu'i Tonga clean but remain or leftover', possibly a symbol for an oppressive TT; married and resided in Samoa[14].

Ma'a means clean and katoe means left overs possibly of food. Can also mean, ma'a or for Katoe possibly a person. 'The King favors Katoe'[17].

Tu'i Tonga Ma'akatoe may have been the name used in Samoa. In Tonga it would have simply been Ma'akatoe[17].

The children of Ma'akatoe[10] was;

1. Puipuifatu

Tu'i Tonga 18

Puipuifatu

He was known as Tu'i Tonga Puipui meaning Tu'i Tonga the secluded, symbolically signify divine character of TT; married and resided in Samoa[14].

Could also mean being covered. Residing in Samoa may have been as a form of protection[17].

Puipuifatu[10] is another name which could be the Tongan name with Tu'i Tonga Puipui used in Samoa[17].

The children of Puipuifatu was;

1. Havea TT 19

Tu'i Tonga 19

Havea I

Havea I was assassinated by a Fijian[1] at his favorite pool, Tolopona[10], 'Alakifonua. Tolopona is a pool of supposedly cool, fresh water gushing out from the rocks into the sea at the beach about 100 metres from the landing place of Captain James Cook[17], when he attended and witnessed the 'Inasi on 30th April, 1777.

Probably symbolic of Tongan recognition of the role of Samoa, in terms of "Savea" (Samoan version of Havea), in local politics; murdered possibly by Fijian, suggesting Fijian opposition to TT imperial rule[14].

The children of Havea I[10] were;

1. Tatafu'eikimeimu'a TT20
2. Ngana

Tu'i Tonga 20

Tatafu'eikimeimu'a

Tatafu means scrape up the earth then clap the hands (the Tongan words tata and fu) , possibly reflecting hou'eiki-tu'a servility; 'eiki-mei Mu'a or high chief from Mu'a or Tatafu the highchief from Mu'a[14].

Scraping up the earth and clap the hands, to get dust off, is associated with fei'umu or earth oven cooking, supposedly the lowest of profession connected with tu'a or commoner, and major undertaking such as building of langi, probable symbolic reference to oppression[14].

TT20 had two sons, Ngana'eiki (is also another name for Tatafu'eikimeimu'a[10]) and Nganatatafu; Ngana'eiki means befitting a chief, unsuccessfully courted a Samoan princess, Hina, who fell in love with his younger more handsome brother, Nganatatafu[14].

Nganatatafu and Hina had a son, Malupo'atonga who became the first Malupo ancestor of the Lord Malupo of 'Uiha and Lord Tu'i Ha'angana of Ha'ano lines of present day Kingdom of Tonga[10].

The name Ongoha'angana originate from these brothers and used to refer to 'Uiha and Ha'ano in Tongan ancient oratory[17].

The children of Tatafu'eikimeimu'a was:

1. Lomi'aetupu'a TT 21

Tu'i Tonga 21

Lomi'aetupu'a

Lomi'aetupu'a means 'suppression of the ancient/past. Little is known about this TT, name may symbolically represent counter-hegemony against the TT, ancient symbol of power[14].

The children of Lomi'aetupu'a was:

1. Havea II, TT22

Tu'i Tonga 22

Havea II

Havea II also assassinated by a Fijian named Tuluvota[10].

Samoan influences in terms of "Savea"; Havea II was murdered by Fijian, Tuluvota, pointing to further Fijian oppositional encounters to TT imperialism[14].

The children of Havea II was;

1. Takalaua TT23

Tu'i Tonga 23

Takalaua

Takalaua was King at about 1375 AD (CE). His name means 'all around gossip'; may be symbolic of suppression being the subject of much dissatisfied "talks" by subjects or colonies. Takalaua extended imperial rule beyond Fiji and Samoa to Futuna and 'Uvea, and possibly Niue, Tokelau and Tuvalu. Imperial expansion reached perhaps to Polynesian outliers such as Tikopia and Anuta in Melanesia and places such as the Cooks and the Marquesas in Eastern Polynesia; 'Uvean and Futunan inspired murder by Tamasia and Malofafa for reputed oppression; virtual end of imperial expansion by conquest-alliance formation[14].

Takalaua was murdered during the kava ceremony at an island known as Mata'aho in the Tongatapu lagoon. Tamasia and

Malofafa belonged to the Ha'a Talafale. Kau'ulufonua and his siblings were swimming on the beach when Va'elaveamata, the favorite wife of Takalaua, came heartbroken with the sad news that their father had been murdered. Kau'ulufonua replied that it is new to hear of the king being killed. The place where they swam was called Talafo'ou[10] or 'new news', 'astonishing report' or 'shocking report'[17]. Kau'ulufonua and his siblings made a vow they will not bury their father until Tamasia and Malofafa are caught and punished. They chased them through Ha'apai, Vava'u, Niua, Samoa, 'Uvea and caught them at Futuna. They were bound and brought back to Tonga where they were forced to chew the kava root for the kava ceremony. Then their bodies were chopped up and cooked as fono or food for the partakers in the kava ceremony. Kau'ulufonua was known from that time as Kau'ulufonuafekai or Kau'ulufonua the 'ferocius eater of men'[10].

The children of Takalaua[10] were:

1. Kau'ulufonua TT24

2. Mo'ungamotu'a TH1
3. Melino'atonga
4. Lotau'ai
5. Latutoevave

They were the children of Va'elaveamata.

6. Takalaua

His mother is unknown.

Tu'i Tonga 24

Kau'ulufonua

Kau'ulufonua also known as Kau'ulufonuafekai in Tonga and Fasi'atele in Samoa[10]. The name means 'combining all lands/islands' may be symbolic of extensive imperialism, attempts to regain imperial control; began imperial expansion by alliance formation; major social reforms: reorganised Falefa; created Tu'i Ha'a Takalaua; sent out chiefs as governors to outer islands; laid down foundation for polopolo and 'inasi institutions, linked with Fahu and 'Ulumotu'a[14].

The new arrangement by Kau'ulufonua to protect the Kings in the future was to establish a new line of kings as protector of the Tu'i Tonga and the country. He installed his younger brother Mo'ungamotu'a as the first king of that line known as the Ha'a Takalaua or Takalaua Clan after his father. His youngest brother, Takalaua, was sent as Governor of 'Eua. Kolomoe'uto and Mata'uvave were sent as governors to Ha'apai. Haveatuli and Niutongo were sent as governors to Vava'u. Talapalo was sent to Niuatoputapu and Matauka and Hakauvalu were installed as governors in Niuafo'ou. 'Elili was sent as governor of 'Uvea[10].

The Governor names were also hereditary titles[10].

This account of the killing of Tamasia and Malofafa is a graphic tale of the ferociousness of Kau'ulufonua[1].

Kau'ulufonua I[1] – ruled around 1470, pursued his father's murderers from Tongatapu to 'Eua, Ha'apai, Vava'u, both Niuas, then Niue, Fiji, Samoa, finally arresting them at their home island of either 'Uvea or Futuna. Back at home in Mu'a he killed them in a savage spectacle (knocking out their teeth and then letting them chew kava), before he cooked and devoured them giving him the nickname *fekai*. He installed his younger brother Moʻungāmotuʻa as founder of the new dynasty, the Tuʻi Haʻatakalaua, named after their father. This new dynasty would carry out the day-to-day duties of the Tuʻi Tonga with the people while the Tuʻi Tonga became sacred, king of kings like a god.

The children of Kau'ulufonua[10] were;

1. Vakafuhu TT25
2. Tuiavi'i
3. Togialelei

Their mother is a maiden by the name of Popo'ai from Samoa

4. Puipuifatu II TT26

His mother is a maiden by the name of Toafaitoa from Samoa

5. Kau'ulufonua II, TT27
6. Ulualofaiga
7. Poluleuligaga

Their mother is a maiden by the name of
Vainu'ulasi from Samoa.

Tu'i Tonga 25

Vakafuhu

Vakafuhu kept away from Tonga by the Tu'i Ha'atakalaua, lived in Samoa[1]. Vakafuhu means 'boat of fighters', probable symbolic reference to Kau'ulufonua's fleet of fighting men that pursued his father's murderers; exiled and married in Samoa[14].

The children of Vakafuhu[10] was;

1. Tu'itofua 1

His mother is Langitaetaea

Tu'i Tonga 26

Puipuifatu II

Puipuifatu II is the younger brother of Vakafuhu, lived in Samoa, tried in vain to invade Vava'u to restore power to his dynasty[1] means secluded offspring; probable symbol for this divine TT exile and marriage in Samoa[14].

The children of Puipuifatu II[10] was:

1. Laufilitonga

Laufilitonga liked Vava'u and resided there thus becoming the first great chief of Vava'u. Laufilitonga's son was Lolomana'ia the ancestor of the Lord Tu'i'afitu line.

Tu'i Tonga 27

Kau'ulufonua II

Kau'ulufonua II lived in Samoa[1], in exile and married in Samoa[14]

The children of Kau'ulufonua II was;

1. Tapu'osi TT28

Note - since the establishment of the Tu'i Ha'a Takalaua by the 24rd Tu'i Tonga Kau'ulufonua as a protector of the Tu'i Tonga, many of the later Tu'i Tonga spent much of their time in Samoa. One theory was 1. it was a protective measure during internal unrest in Tonga, the other theory was 2. that the Tu'i Ha'a Takalaua was too powerful and the office of the Tu'i Tonga was often exiled especially if there was disagreement or even a war between the two. In some cases, the Tu'i Ha'a Takalaua challenged the Tu'i Tonga and won, in some cases a 'one on one' or 'hand to hand' combat.

Tu'i Tonga 28

Tapu'osi

Tapu'osi was allowed to return to Mu'a, as apparently the Tu'i Tonga line was now so weakened as to be of no threat to the Tu'i Ha'atakalaua. From now on the Tu'i Tonga functioned as a kind of high priest, taking care of all religious obligations (an honour and a burden), giving him a very elevated status, but no worldly power. No Tu'i Tonga was ever murdered anymore either[1].

The name Tapu'osi means 'prohibition is lifted' or 'tapu has ended', may be symbolically representative of TT having completed terns of exile in Samoa; Tapu'osi I, suggesting Fijian role in Tongan politics, last to have married and resided in Samoa[14.]

Tapu'osi took Va'etapu, daughter of
'Ahome'e of Ha'avakatolo, as his wife
and they had a son 'Uluakimata I or
Tele'a TT29[10].

Tu'i Tonga 29

Uluakimata I

'Uluakimata I was also known as Tele'a, builder of the greatest langi on Tongatapu[1], known as the Paepae 'o Tele'a. This King was the owner of the famed legendary gigantic canoe known as the Lomipeau reputed to have brought stones from 'Uvea for the building the langi[10]. There are 28 langi or burial pyramids in the ancient capital of Mu'a, some of which were built with sand stone slabs mined at Pangaimotu, Makaha'a and Fafa Islands off the coast of Tongatapu[1].

The name 'Uluakimata means 'first face/eye'[14] or 'original people/occupants'[17], possibly symbolic of this TT being the "first" to restore some kind of respectable "face" to TT rule; Tele'a (Valley), a reference to Mu'a, TT "valleys"; connected with huge legendary double-canoe, kalia, Lomipeau[14].

The name Tele'a was probably added later when 'Uluakimata cut a huge canal inland and flooded it with seawater for bringing the canoes closer to the building sites. This canal is still visible at Lapaha village on the main roadside although without water, and probably filled in over the last 400 years or so. The depth of the excavation could have made it look like a tele'a or valley. The depth of the great canal is still very impressive at around 10 metres or so[17].

'Uluakimata's favorite wife was the notorious and beautiful Talafaiva, MTH1 , known as the first Moheofo from the Ha'a Takalaua line.

The children of 'Uluakimata with Talafaiva[10] was;

1. 'Eikifietu'a

'Uluakimata also had Nanasilapaha as his second wife with no recorded children.

'Uluakimata had a third wife, Mata'ukipa, daughter of Kau'ulufonua huo and they had 3 children[10];

1. Sinaitakala'ilangilekaTTF3
2. Fatafehi TT30
3. 'Uliafu

Tu'i Tonga 30

Fatafehi

Fatafehi ruled around 1600, married the 6th Tu'i Ha'atakalaua Mo'ungatonga's daughter, a custom which would last for some generations to come forming a permanent alliance between the two houses; his sister married a Fijian, changing the international orientation of Tonga from Samoa to Fiji. Was tattooed in Samoa by master tattooists in two sessions and received the nickname Fakauakimanuka ("Twice to Manu'a") in commemoration of these rituals[1].

The name Fatafehi means litter? of fehi wood'[14] or 'bearer/carrier box made of fehi wood' or 'attic made of fehi wood'[17], a chiefly symbol, contemporaneous with emergence of female social institutions of Moheofo, Tu'i Tonga Fefine and Tamaha vis-a-vis TT, and collateral segmentation of third kingly line, TK[14].

Fatafehi's favorite wife or moheofo was Kaloafutonga, MTH2. Second Moheofo from the Ha'a Takalaua line.

The children of Fatafehi include[10*];

(*-reference James Cocker acknowledged his source of most information is the book of genealogy by Fohe Ma'afutakinima written in 1903, although he added many of the references from his own research).

1. Siufanga
2. Inu
3. Fatafehi 'Atalua

Their mother was Alaitokaloto, daughter of Va'etu'ikoloa, sister of Mo'ungatonga TH6.

4. 'Eukitongapipiki TTF4
5. Kau'ulufonua III TT31
6. Luavava'u

The mother is Kaloafutonga MTH2, koe 'ofefine 'o Mo'ungatonga TH6

Tu'i Tonga 31

Kau'ulufonua III

(also known as Tapu'osi II)

Kau'ulufonua III was the King who met Abel Tasman in 1643[1].

Tapu'osi is suggestive of more Fijian influences on Tonga; lived around the time of Tasman's visit in 1643[14].

Kau'ulufonua IIIs favorite wife and MTH3 was Takalalahi daughter of Fotofili TH7 and 'Atalua.

The children of Kau'ulufonua[10] were;

1. 'Uluakimata II TT32
2. Totonukuo'osi

The mother is Takalalahi, MTH3.

3. Tafololahi ,Tafolo 1
4. Fatafehi

The mother is Tu'utangahunuhunu, daughter of
Atamata'ila TK2 and Tokilupe.

5. Simuoko Tu'e

The mother is Tae.

6. Tavui, Hama 1

This King was also known as Tapu'osi II.

Tu'i Tonga 32

'Uluakimata II

Ulakimata II's two sons, Tu'ipulotu-'i-Langi-Tu'ofefafa TT33 and Tokemoana I, started the Tu'i Ha'a 'Uluakimata line[14].

There were only 5 title holders in the Tokemoana line which bore the title Tu'i Ha'a 'Uluakimata[17]. The last Tokemoana, Tokemoana V was the older brother of 'Ulukalala II (Tu'i Vava'u) and Tupouto'a (Tu'i Ha'apai, TK17) having the same mother to 'Ulukilupetea[21] daughter of Tu'i Ha'apai Ngalumotutulu who was the son of Ma'afu 'o Tu'i Tonga TK6. It is possible Tokemoana V died in the battle of Velata in 1827 and his title abolished because he was fighting on the Tu'i Tonga Laufilitonga's side which lost the second battle[17]. It is noted in several references that it was probably Tokemoana V[17], the paramount chief of Ha'apai, who brought,

Laufilitonga the Tu'i Tonga, there to oppose the ambitions of Taufa'ahau son of his younger brother Tupouto'a[17].

There are some views that the Tu'i Ha'a 'Uluakimata was never installed again after the death of the first Tu'i Ha'a 'Uluakimata, Tokemoana I, possibly because Tokemoana II resided mostly in Samoa and was known as Tokemoana'iHa'amoa. He had a Samoan mother.

His younger brother was installed to the title Tokemoana III[17]. The full story of Tokemoana is covered later in the stories section at the back of this book.

The favorite wife of 'Uluakimata II was Toa the fourth Moheofo from the Ha'a Takalaua line. Toa was the daughter of Vaeatangitauki'uvea,TH8 and Taumoe[10].

The children were[10];

1. Tu'ipulotu'ilangitu'ofefafa TT33
2. Tokemoana 1, Tu'iha'a'uluakimata 1
3. Faleafa

4. Fatani

5. Sinaitakala'ilotunofo, TTF5

Mother of the first five children was Toa.

6. Pahihi, Tu'iha'ateiho 1

The mother was 'Uno'unoa, a surrogate wife[17+]
from Toa.

(+ - surrogate wives or fokonofo were sisters, cousins or
nieces of the moheofo who stand in when she is indisposed,
for example when she has her menstruation period and is
unavailable).

7. Tu'ihoua

8. Finaule'o

The mother was Longo, younger sister and
surrogate wife from Toa.

9. Pahulu

Mother is unknown[10], probably one of the
surrogate wives from Toa[17].

Tu'i Tonga 33

Tu'ipulotu 'i Langitu'ofefafa

(also known as Tu'ipulotu I)

Tu'ipulotu 'ilangi tu'ofefafa began the moheofo dynasty. From now on the Tu'i Tonga principal wife *(moheofo)* became the daughter of the Tu'i Kanokupolu instead of the Tu'i Ha'atakalaua, showing which dynasty of the latter two was now the most important[1].

The idea behind the moheofo was to transfer the divinity, power and paramount status of the Tu'i Tonga to the Tu'i Kanokupolu through the heir who is now the grandson of the Tu'i Kanokupolu. This very important link puts the Tu'i Tonga under the Tu'i Kanokupolu lineage[17].

This King was also known as Tu'ipulotu I[1].

The name of Tu'ipulotu'ilangitu'ofefafa
means 'kings of Pulotu who are buried on
top of each other at the langi Tu'ofefafa' ;
so named for reasons that he was buried
face down with his brother, Tokemoana,
on his back; Pulotu/Fisi suggests further
Fijian penetration in Tongan affairs[14].

The favorite or principal wife of
Tu'ipulotu was the first moheofo from the
Tu'i Kanokupolu suggesting a shift in
power from the Tu'i Ha'a Takalaua[17]. She
was Halaevalu, MTK1 or first Moheofo
from the Tu'i Kanokupolu, daughter of
Mataeleha'amea TK4 and Kaloafutonga,
but there were no children[10].

A first surrogate wife from Halaevalu,
Taufa, daughter of Halaevalu's uncle,
Kafoamotalau TH 11 and Totonukuo'osi
did not bear any children

The children of Tu'ipulotu[10] with the
surrogate wives were;

1. Fakana'ana'a, TT34

His mother was Manuna, surrogate wife from
Halaevalu

Manuna was the daughter of Kavamo'unga'one
and Heimoana of Mo'unga'one.

2. Peseta
3. Fatafehiha'amea

Their mother was Fakatoumafi, daughter of
'Itafua'a'atonga and 'Evaipomana. 'Itafua'a'atonga
was the son of Kinikinilaulahi and
Fotuihalatata. Kinikilaulahi was the son of
Fotofili TH7.

Tu'i Tonga 34

Fakana'ana'a

The name Fakana'ana'a means a lullaby[14] and can also mean to 'soothe from crying'; probably symbolic of local Fijian influences via the "crying" Sinaitakala-'ilangileka, who is said to have fakana 'ana'a by her female attendants for falling in love with Tapu'osi. See the story of Sinaitakala'ilangileka in the stories section at the end of this book.

The favorite or principal wife of Fakana'ana'a was Tongotea'ivai, second Moheofo, MTK2, daughter of Mataele Ha'amea TK4 and Humi Fakamolefonua[17] (or Fakavalefonua[10])

The children[10] were;

1. Tu'ipulotu'ilangitu'oteau, TT35

2. Sinaitakala'ifanakavakilangi, TTF6
3. Hahanokifanga'uta

The mother is Tongotea'ivai.

4. Sisifa, Fohe 2

The mother was Toa'afilimoe'unga, daughter of
Fohe 1 who was a surrogate wife from
Tongotea'ivai.

5. Laufilitonga
6. Manuna

The mother was Fifita, another surrogate wife
from Tongotea'ivai. Fifita was the daughter of
Longolongo'atumai son of Mataeletu'apiko TK3
with Tu'imala, Tamaha 1.

7. Mafi'uli'uli
8. Fakatoumafi
9. Tupuivao
10. Tapu'osi

The mother was Lupemoetavake, daughter of
Tau'atevalu, Valu 4, of 'Utulau and Funaki Falefa.

Tu'i Tonga 35

Tu'ipulotu'ilangitu'oteau

(also known as Tu'ipulotu II)

Tu'ipolutu'ilangi Tu'oteau was also known as Tu'ipulotu II[1].

The name of Tu'ipulotu'iLangiTu'oteau means 'king of Pulotu who is buried in the tomb with the hundred layers'. Mahina suggests that this is evident of further Fijian influences on local Tongan politics[14].

The name could also mean having 'relations or sex for a hundred times' [17] which could be a reason why this king had so many children. The name Longolongo'atumai, one of the surrogate wives of Fakana'ana'a is suggestive of 'quiet meetings for the purpose of having sex at night-time', the meaning of the name. Longolongo is 'being quiet' and 'atumai' means 'I give you and you return it' suggestive of intercourse or penetration of the female by the male[17]. It could also mean that male visits to the female's house is reciprocated by the female visiting the male's house for the purpose of having sex. Many of the visitors to Tonga had made the observation that Tongan women were promiscuous in nature[23], but we know it is part of the ancient culture. The provision of women to kings, chiefs and leaders were compulsory as evident in the practice of providing surrogate wives when the principal wife cannot provide for the king's sexual requirements[17].

In some of George Vason[22] of the London Missionary Society records, the nature of the King's house was such that there may be more than one person sleeping there and any discreet affairs has to be done quietly. George Vason spent 4 years in Tonga from 1797 and his book was the first ever book published about Tonga in

1810 followed by William Mariner's book in 1817[17].

The principal wife of Tu'ipulotu'ilangitu'oteau TT35 was Tu'ilokamana, MTK3 or third Moheofo from the Tu'i Kanokupolu, daughter of Vuna TK5 and Lahauku.

The children[10] were;

1. Alaivahamama'o
2. Ta'emoemimi
3. Nanasipau'u TTF8

Mother was Tu'ilokamana, MTK3.

4. Manumataongo
5. Ma'ulupekotofa TT37
6. Fatafehi Fehu'iameipulotu
7. Fakaolakifanga

Mother was 'Anaukihesina, surrogate wife from Tu'ilokamana. 'Anaukihesina was the daughter of Ma'afuotu'itonga TK6 and Latutama III.

7. Pau'uli

Mother is unknown.

9. Paulaho TT36
10. Talaumokafoa
11. Mapafisi Avatongo
12. Siumafua'uta TTF7

Mother was Laumanukilupe, another surrogate
wife from Tu'ilokamana. Laumanukilupe was the
daughter of Tupouto'a[17*] and Longosi'i.

(* - This Tupouto'a is probably the son of Mataele
Ha'amea TK4, not to be confused with Tupouto'a son of
Tuku'aho, TK14)

13. Tuki'ao

Mother was Tangaloa, another surrogate wife
from Tu'ilokomana. Tangaloa was the daughter
of Mataelemuluvala, son of Vuna TK5.

14. Laufilitongakakau.

Mother was Tupouta'anea, another surrogate wife
from Tu'ilokamana. Tupouta'anea was the
daughter of Vuna TK5 with Halaevaluta'anea.

15. Fatafehi Manupupui'one

Mother was Fakatoumafi, daughter of Tu'ihoua
and Heuifanga.

16. Hiliaunifo

Mother was Lapuloufisi, daughter of
Fehokomoelangifisi, Tu'ilakepa 4 and
Sinaitakala'ifanakavakilangi TTF6.

17. Sisifa

Mother was Hafuni.

18. Tupoupau'u

Mother was Ma'ulahi, daughter of
Langiloa Lauaki and Ma'avamokahokaho.

19. Sisifa

Mother was Puakatefisi, daughter of Tupouto'a
and Afeaki.

Tu'i Tonga 36

Paulaho

(also known as Paulahi or Pau)

Paulaho or Pau had very strong Fijian influences, Pau was probably named after Bau in Fiji; Paulaho which means ' Pau the testicle', a probable recording error, married Tupoumoheofo, daughter of TK7 Tupoulahi. Pau reported to have **'kisu e tala e fonua'**, withheld body of refined knowledge of ruling from his son, Fatafehi Fuanunuiava[14].

Fuanunuiava, was his successor during a grand ceremony in 1777, witnessed by Captain Cook; was defeated and deposed in a following civil war[1].

There is another variant of Pau's name which is Paulahau, mentioned in some records[17] (but could also be mispronounced by visitors as Polahau or even Pohahau) and even Paulahi or 'Pau the elder', which suggested there was a Pau jr although not in the records[17].

The children of Pau[10] were;

1. Sinaitakala'ifekitetele TTF9
2. Fatafehiolapaha TTF10
3. Fatafehiha'apai
4. Manutauhakau
5. Fatafehi Fuanunu'iava TT38

The mother is Tupoumoheofo, MTK4. She was also installed as 12th TK. Tupoumoheofo was the daughter of Tupoulahimu'a TK7 and Fuonuku. See story of Tupou Moheofo in the stories of the Tu'i Tonga era at the end of this book.

6. Fatafehitoutai
7. Ikatulifota
8. Fatafehivava'u

The mother was Inumofalefa, who was a surrogate wife from Tupoumoheofo.

9. Fatafehimatamoana

The mother was Palu, a surrogate wife from Tupoumoheofo. Palu was the daughter of Fufuutauma'a, son of Tupouto'a (son of Mataele Ha'amea TK4[17]) and Kilinganoa (daughter of Tokemoana I).

10. Likutauifangatapu

Mother was Kongakava, daughter of Maealiuaki TH15, TK8 and Langilangiha'aluma (daughter of Teukihe'alo'i or Ve'ehala II and Tangakinatofetofe, daughter of Nuku Hape or Nuku III and Ngaosi'i).

11. Fatafehi
12. Sinalauli'i

Mother was Pulimaipau, daughter of Latuniupulu'iteafua or Tu'ilakepa V and Tongavua, daughter of Talia'ulilahi or Talia'uli I and Vui.

13. Fifitavakaniua
14. Sisifa

Mother was Fifitavakaniua, daughter of
Haveatunguamata'uli and Finaulangi.

Tu'i Tonga 37

Ma'ulupekotofa

Ma'ulupekotofa was the older brother of Paulaho, who should have been Tu'i Tonga in the first place without Paulaho; tried to reduce the burden of religious taboos grown on the Tu'i Tonga and to increase its political influence[1].

Ma'ulupekotofa lived between AD 1784-AD 1806. His name means 'pigeon for the royal sleep' (or pigeon for the royal bed [17]) probably allegorical of women being presented to cohabit with the TT[14].
The principal wife of Ma'ulupekotofa was Mo'ungaolakepa, daughter of Fehokomoelangifisi or Tu'ilakepa 4 and Sinaitakala'ifanakavakilangi TTF6.
Ma'ulupe and Mo'unga'olakepa did not have any children.

The children of Ma'ulupekotofa[10] were;

1. Fatafehifisi

Mother was Lupe'utulau, daughter of Tamalepau'u son of Tau'atevalu or Valu of 'Utulau.

2. Papani

Mother was Halavaivai, daughter of 'Umufeke and Latutama, daughter of Tu'ikolovatu.

Tu'i Tonga 38

Fuanunu'iava

Fuanunu'iava took the power from his uncle, Ma'ulupekotofa, in or around 1795, but continued his policy; joined Fīnau 'Ulukālala in the civil war of 1799; died in 1810[1].

Fatafehi Fuanunuiava was reported to have been installed to the 38th TT while Pau was still alive. He was the TT from 1806 - 1810[14] (probably or more likely to be 1795 to 1810[17]).

This may have been the influence and plan of his mother Tupou Moheofo, who also had herself installed as TK 12[17].The principal wife of Fuanunu'iava was Tupoufalemei, MTK5 (daughter of Tu'ihalafatai TK9 and Laavaka daughter of 'Ahovalu). Another prinicipal wife was Tupouveiongo, daughter of Mumui

Mapatongia'amanu TK13 and
Tulehu'afaikikava, adopted daughter
of Motu'apuaka).

The children of Fuanunu'iava[10] were;

1. Kafaikamoana

Mother was Mo'ungaotupou, daughter of
Tongamana and Siumafua'uta TTF7.

2. Mo'ungaotupou
3. Hu'akavamei'uiha
4. Kavafutuna

Mother was Tupoufalemei 5th TK Moheofo
(daughter of Mulikiha'amea TH16, TK6 and
Teuteufaiva another adopted daughter of
Motu'apuaka).

5. Manumapuhola

Mother was Palulongoteme, surrogate wife from
Tupoufalemei.

6. Laufilitonga TT39.
7. Lataimaumi.

Mother was Tupouveiongo 6th TK Moheofo

(daughter of Mumui
Mapatongia'amanu TK13 and Tulehu'afaikikava,
adopted daughter of Motu'apuaka).

8. Fatafehi

Mother was Popua, surrogate wife from
Tupouveiongo. Popua was the daughter of Finau
'Ulukalala or 'Ulukalala I and Adi Vuturongo of
Lakeba, Fiji.

9. Hake'ivaiha'akili
10. Fatafehimei

Mother was Finauha'akili, surrogate wife from
Tupouveiongo.

11. Fatafehiha'apai

Mother was Finau, surrogate wife from
Tupouveiongo.

Tu'i Tonga 39

Laufilitonga

Laufilitonga was born around 1798 and was too young to become Tu'i Tonga when his father died in 1810; by that time the title had so declined as to have lost almost all prestige; tried to opt for power, but lost the final battle
at Velata on Lifuka in 1826
against Tāufa'āhau; was 'mockingly*' installed as Tu'i Tonga in 1827 as a king with neither political nor spiritual power; died in 1865 after which the title was abolished[1].

* - there are many references to Laufilitonga being installed as a 'joke' but I would like to point out these obligations which were still carried out despite his

being 'mockingly' installed as Tu'i
Tonga[17].

First, the supply of wives to the Tu'i
Tonga were still carried out, although it is
noted that the term moheofo was no
longer used. For example, in the case of
Luseane Halaevalu Mata'aho, daughter of
the TK17 Tupouto'a, she was given as a
wife to Laufilitonga but was never
referred to as moheofo in all the literature
I have read.

Secondly, the office of the Tu'i Tonga
was still held in the highest regard and his
descendants are revered and
acknowledged today, some 156 years later.

Thirdly, it is never mentioned as if the
silence is evidence itself, the 10 years
from the death of the last Tu'i Tonga,
Laufilitonga (1865), to the establishment
of the Kingdom of Tonga (1875) is almost
an observance of the passing of a Tu'i
Tonga as in ancient times.

I would propose that the Tu'i Tonga
Laufilitonga was installed in 1827 despite

the loss in the second battle at Velata in 1826, because the office of the Tu'i Tonga still commanded more respect than any other line of kings[17].

Laufilitonga[14] - his name means 'make a decision and choose Tonga'[17] . It might have been a challenge to Vava'u and Ha'apai, may represent , symbolic position of Tongatapu[14] (as the sacred seat of power[17]) and structural-functional relationships (between the islands[17]) . That is between secular Hau, TH and TK and 'Eiki, for example TT spent most of his time in Vava'u and Ha'apai but elected to live in Tongatapu during last days of his life; defeated by TK in battle; died in 1865[14].

The children of Laufilitonga[10] were;

1. Manumataongo Lutoviko

Mother was Latuniua, daughter of Kahomovailahi or Tuita and Latufu'ipeka, 2nd Tamaha.

2. Viliami Fatafehiolapaha (Kalaniuvalu 1)
3. Lavinia Veiongo

Mother was Luseane Halaevalu Mata'aho, daughter of Tupouto'a TK17 and Tupou'ahome'e (daughter of Tupoulahisi'i TK10 and Latufu'ipeka 2nd Tamaha).

4. Tu'ipulotupau'u Losaline Fonofaa
5. Panuve Manumapuhola
6. Fatafehifanga'afa

Mother was Siulolovao, daughter of Sisitoutai and Fataimoemanu Fotofili. Sisitoutai was the son of Toutaitokotaha or Tokemoana 4 and Fifitaha'amotuku who was known as Popaofehi. Fataimoemanu was the daughter of 'Aloko'ulu or Fotofili I.

7. Tu'ifangatukia Hepisipa.

Mother was Latufakahau Kelesi, daughter of Tu'ihalafatai TK9? and Mafikakau (daughter of Finakikalava or Fakafanua and Fotuihalatala).

8. Kafaikamoana
9. Fatafehi
10. Nanasi

Mother was Popuamoholeva.

11. Latuholeva

Mother was Manu, surrogate wife from older sister Latufakahau Kelesi, she was the daughter of Tu'ihalafatai TK9 and Latuholeva.

12. Mahetuputau

Mother was Sovaki, daughter of Talanoa and Taufa. Talanoa is the son of Mumui Mapatongiaamanu TK13 and Kaingama'uvaka. Taufa was the daughter of Ikafililava daughter of Ma'afu II and Fualupeake.

13. Tupoutu'a Lamanukilupe.

Mother was Fala'aetau, daughter of Tupoumonukunuku and Ngingie. (Tupoumonukunuku is the son of Hiliaunifo son

of Tu'ipulotu'ilangitu'oteau TT35. Ngingie is a
daughter of Tongamana and Taetaeveve.
Tongamana is a son of Tupoulahimu'a TK7 and
Lupemeitakui).

14. Fe'aomoemanu'okotone

The mother was Tapapala, daughter of
Tu'ihafatai TK 9? and Mafikakau. Tapapala was
a surrogate wife from older sister Latufakahau
Kelesi.

15. Fatafehi Kulivolivoli
16. Fatafehi Fakauakimanu'a

The mother was Fusi Kilisitina, daughter of
Talia'ulimalohi and Fusipapalangi.

17. Salesi Tu'ipulotu Langitu'oteau

The mother is Mafikakau, daughter of
'Itafua'a'atonga or Fakafanua 4 and Levanuia,
daughter of Tongotea and Na'asipa. (Tongotea is
a son of Manulevu, son of Fuatakifolaha TH14.
Na'asipa is a daughter of Lupetulimafua Lavaka
of Pea.

18. Kalilea

The mother wasVika Mafi, daughter of Tupouneiafu, son of Maealiuaki ,TH15, TK8 and Langilangiha'aluma.

19. Toafilimoe'unga

The mother was Va'e (Va'etapu?).

20. Alo Filisonu'u.

The mother is Takala.

21. Tupoutulikihakautapu

The mother was Mo'unga'ulufeholoi, daughter of Moimoiangaha or Nuku 7 and Kavafutuna, daughter of Tupoulahisi'i TK10 and Fusipala Ha'atauele, daughter of Fa'oa.

22. Tupoumanakofo'ufa'u

The mother was Nauvale.

23. Tonga

The mother was Lahauku, daughter of Tu'imakite, son of Lolomana'ia Tu'i'afitu and Toaafilimoe'unga, daughter of Mataeletu'apiko TK3 and Papaha'amea.

24. Taungapuaka

The mother was Mohulamu Filiahihifo.

Important titles of the Tu'i Tonga Era and the office holders

1. Tamaha

The female Tamaha was the highest ranked person in ancient Tonga, second only to the male Tamaha known as Tamatauhala but there was only one, Makamalohi, in recorded history. Usually the Tamaha is a child of the Female Tu'i Tonga and the Tu'i Lakepa or chief of similar rank.

(i) Tamaha 1 (First Tamaha) - Tu'imala
(ii) Tamaha 2 (Second Tamaha) - Latufu'ipeka

2. Tu'i Tonga Fefine (Female Tu'i Tonga)

(i) First Female Tu'i Tonga was Latutama

Daughter of Momo, 10th Tu'i Tonga and Nua.

(ii) Fatafehi

Daughter of Tu'itatui, 11th Tu'i Tonga and Latutama TTF1 (his own sister)

(iii) Sinaitakala'ilangileka

Daughter of 'Uluakimata I, 29th Tu'i Tonga and Mata'ukipa.

(iv) 'Eukitongapipiki

Daughter of Fatafehi 30th Tu'i Tonga and Kaloafutonga, MTH2

(v) Sinaitakala'ilotunofo

Daughter of 'Uluakimata II, 32nd Tu'i Tonga with Toa MTH4.

(vi) Sinaitakala'ifanakavakilangi

Daughter of Fakana'ana'a 34th Tu'i Tonga and Tongotea'ivai MTK2.

(vii) Siumafua'uta

Daughter of Tu'ipulotu'ilangitu'oteau, 35th Tu'i Tonga and Laumanukilupe, surrogate wife from Tu'ilokomana MTK3.

(viii) Nanasipau'u

Daughter of Tu'ipulotu'ilangitu'oteau, 35th Tu'i Tonga and Tu'ilokomana, MTK3.

(ix) Sinaitakala'ifekitetele

Daughter of Pau, 36th Tu'i Tonga and
Tupoumoheofo 12TK

(x) Fatafehi 'o Lapaha

Daughter of Pau, 36th Tu'i Tonga and
Tupoumoheofo 12TK

3. Moheofo of the Tu'i Ha'a Takalaua (MTH)

(i) First Moheofo from Tu'i Ha'a Takalaua - Talafaiva

Daughter of Siulangapo, 4th Tu'i Ha'a Takalaua,
mother is not known possibly Samoan. There is a
story that when Talafaiva was killed by 'Auka for
her disloyal dalliance with Lolomana'ia, her
Samoan relatives took her to Manu'a for burial
but 'Uluakimata, was heartbroken and followed.
He tried to bring her body back to Tonga and
legend suggest he died in Manu'a while trying to
bring her back.

(ii) MTH 2 - Kaloafutonga

Daughter of Mo'ungatonga 6th Tu'i Ha'a
Takalaua with Maholokuku.

(iii) MTH 3 - Takalahi

Daughter of Fotofili, 7th Tu'i Ha'a Takalaua with Fatafehi 'Atalua, granddaughter of Vakalahi Mohe'uli TH5.

(iv) MTH 4 - Toa

Daughter of Vaeatangitauki'uvea, TH8 and Taumoe daughter of 'Atamata'ila, TK2.

4. Moheofo of the Tu'i Kanokupolu (MTK)

(i) The first Moheofo of the Tu'i Kanokupolu was Halaevalu

Halaevalu was the daughter of Mataele Ha'amea, TK4 and Kaloafutonga daughter of Vaeatangitauki'uvea, TH8.

(ii) Tongotea'ivai

She was the daughter of Mataeleha'amea, TK 4 and Humi Fakamolefonua younger sister of Kaloafutonga.

(iii) Tu'ilokomana

She was the daughter of Vuna, TK5 and Lahauku, daughter of Tu'ionukulave, TH12 and Langi, daughter of Kafoamotalau TH11.

(iv) Tupoumoheofo

Tupoumoheofo was the daughter of
Tupoulahimu'a, TK7 and Fuonuku, daughter of
Tokemoana I.

(v) Tupoufalemei

Daughter of Tu'ihalafatai, TK9 and Lavaka,
surrogate wife from Talahiva, principal wife? of
TK 9, daughter of Fu'atakifolaha, TK14 and
Nanasiha'ele.

(vi) Tupouveiongo

Daughter of Mumui Mapatongia'amanu, TK13
and Tulehu'afaikikava, adopted daughter
of Motu'apuaka, but daughter of Ve'ehala 2 and
Tangakinatofetofe, daughter of Nukuhape, Nuku
3 of Kolonga.

Why did the Tu'i Tonga Dynasty End?[17]

The Tu'i Tonga line was abolished after the death of the last Tu'i Tonga, Laufilitonga, in 1865. Depending on which academic records you support, whether the beginning was 950 AD or 450[13, 30]* AD, it would mean that , if you choose the latter, the Tu'i Tonga dynasty lasted 1,570 years[17]. A very long time.

* - the date quoted by 'Ilaiu is around 500-650 AD but it is the author's view that it could easily be 450 or earlier considering the 2nd (48) and 3rd (54) lists of Tu'i Tonga in Figure 1.

Taufa'ahau had gained popularity and support since he became Tu'i Ha'apai. He inherited the title Tu'i Ha'apai from his father Tupouto'a TK17 when he died in 1820. He beat the Tu'i Tonga (Laufilitonga) in the second battle of Velata in 1826[1] and took the political and paramount power off him and also seized his property and wife Salote Lupepau'u.

Taufa'ahau became a Christian in 1831 and took on the Christian name King

George of Tonga, after King George of Great Britain. He also took on the Tu'i Vava'u title when 'Ulukalala III, his first cousin, died in 1833 and Tu'i Kanokupolu title in 1845 when Tupou[1] (Aleamotu'a) , his uncle, died.

By 1865, King George of Tonga was also in control of a Parliament he established in 1862[1], and all of the country.

There is also a story that a vote was held by the Chiefs and title holders of Tonga, after the Tu'i Tonga died. It was to choose a new king[17].

There were 4 candidates;

1. Tu'i Tonga Candidate represented by Viliami Fatafehi 'o Lapaha oldest son of Laufilitonga (TT39).
2. Tu'i Ha'a Takalaua candidate represented by Halatuituia (Tungi).
3. Tu'i Kanokupolu Candidate represented by Ma'afu son of Tupou (Aleamotu'a), the last Tu'i Kanokupolu.
4. King George of Tonga (Taufa'ahau)

It was obvious that Taufa'ahau had the most support as he had also the support of the Methodist Church where most Tongans worshiped and so King George of Tonga continued as king and established the Kingdom of Tonga in 1875.

STORIES ASSOCIATED WITH THE TU'I TONGA.

The story of Talafaiva

Talafaiva[24] was the daughter of the 4th Tu'i Ha'a Takalaua, Siulangapo. She is said to be the most beautiful woman of her time. As the first Moheofo or principal wife of the Tu'i Tonga, provided by the second line of kings, the Ha'a Takalaua, Talafaiva was a very important person in Tongan history. She represents the first attempt by the second line of kings to take over the paramount chief title and power of the Tu'i Tonga. Talafaiva also provided 50 surrogate wives[10] for Tele'a from her Ha'a Takalaua relatives.

'Uluakimata had built a separate house for Talafaiva his favorite and principal wife. It had a high fence so no one can come close to her house. However, one day Talafaiva noticed a tree branch growing over the fence and into the compound. She told 'Uluakimata to have the branch removed to prevent anyone climbing into the compound from the outside.

'Uluakimata must have forgotten because the branch was never cut down. One day a young handsome man known as Lolomana'ia came from Vava'u and heard of Talafaiva's beauty. He decided to pay her a visit. Having walked around the fence, there was no way he could get in. There were guards at the gate. He came upon the tree and decided to climb into the compound on the overhanging branch.

Lolomana'ia must have been persuasive with his handsome looks because he became Talafaiva's secret lover. But it wasn't long before the servants and workers noticed him climbing the tree.

Talafaiva's betrayal was reported to the king and legends suggest 'Uluakimata was overcome with anger at his wife's indiscretion. He called his Chief Warrior, 'Auka, and sought his advice. 'Auka informed the king that he will deal with the matter and the king agreed to it, not really specifying what he will do.

As it was in those days, the only penalty for such betrayal of the king is death.

'Auka took his best war club and went to Talafaiva's house and smashed her on the head with it.

The news of what happened reached the king who became very alarmed and rushed to Talafaiva's house. He thought 'Auka would counsel Talafaiva and not kill her, but he was mistaken.

Talafaiva was still alive but the her head wound was fatal. 'Uluakimata asked her why she did it? Talafaiva's answer was 'I told you to remove the tree branch and you did not. Its your own fault', upon which she died.

The king was heartbroken for he had loved Talafaiva very much.

The story is the source of 2 present day proverbs.

1. Koe fo'ui ne fai (It was the tree that caused it). It means something or a problem that befalls somebody because of their own neglect. A reminder of King 'Uluakimata's oversight in not cutting the

tree branch when Talafaiva made the request.

2. Tu'anaki 'Auka (Hopeless 'Auka). This proverb is a reminder of 'Auka's severe punishment when the king was expecting counselling. The deeper meaning is used when you expect someone you had employed or given a task to perform for you and they did a huge disappointing job.

The story of Sinaitakala 'i Langileka

Sinaitakala'ilangileka[24] was the daughter of King 'Uluakimata Tele'a and his third favorite wife, Mata'ukipa. Being the oldest child she became the third female Tu'i Tonga by tradition.

Sinaitakala went to Fiji on a tour with her maidens and when she returned to Mu'a, her relatives noticed that she was looking sick. All the Taula or ancient doctors were consulted but no one was able to find out what is wrong. Sinaitakala was often found crying in her house for no apparent reason. Finally, one of the mid wives noticed tell tale signs that she may be pregnant and the man was probably a Fijian by the name of Tapu'osi.

A kalia was promptly send to Fiji to bring him to Tonga. It was said the man was very hairy and they stopped at Fafa, one of the small islands off the coast of Tongatapu and have all his hair removed. When they arrived at Mu'a, Sinaitakala was overjoyed at seeing Tapu'osi that she became well again and the cause of the ill health was diagnosed.

Tapu'osi became Sinaitakala's husband and was installed as the Tu'i Lakepa, probably after the island he came from in Fiji, Lakemba.

They had a son named Fonomanu. Fonomanu's oldest child was Latu Mailangi who was appointed governor of Niua Toputapu.

Latu Mailangi was the governor who met Shouten and Lemaire, in 1616, the two Dutch sailors were the very first Europeans to land in Tonga. He was the grandson of Sinaitakala and Tapu'osi.

Legend suggest that the name of the 34th Tu'i Tonga, Fakana'ana'a was a reminder of Sinaitakala's miserable days while crying for her lover in Fiji. Fakana'ana'a in Tongan means 'to comfort' or 'to help the person crying to feel better' ....and stop crying.

The story of Mata'ukipa[10]

Mata'ukipa was the third wife of 'Uluakimata Tele'a 29th Tu'i Tonga. Mata'ukipa was known as a Ma'itaki or principal wife of the Tu'i Tonga. The first 2 wives had provided 50 surrogate wives for the king but Mata'ukipa provided a 100.

However, she noticed that during their meals with the king, the first 2 wives got the fish heads and middle part while she and her kids always got the tail end. If it was a pig, they would get the back end of the pig. Mata'ukipa thought that it was an insult to her and her children and one day she could not control her anger, she took her children and left. They went and stayed with Ka'ulufonuahuo, her father, at

Mataliku. Kau'ulufonua was happy to see them but he noticed that after 3 days, there is something wrong.

He inquired as to what is wrong. Mata'ukipa cried and related the story of how they always got the fishtails and back end of the pig.

Kau'ulufonua listened thoughtfully then advised her. The reason why is that her children will be the future Kings of the country and she should go back and take her rightful place as queen.

Mata'ukipa was much encouraged and they returned to the palace and it did happen as Kau'ulufonua predicted. Her son with 'Uluakimata, Fatafehi, became the 30th Tu'i Tonga. Their oldest daughter, Sinaitakala'ilangileka became the 3rd Tu'i Tonga Fefine.

The story of Tokemoana[17]

Tokemoana was the second son of 'Uluakimata II, the 32nd Tu'i Tonga. Tokemoana had 5 children on record[10]; 1. Fuonuku 2. Tokemoana 2 3. Kilinganoa 4. Kaumalu 5. Tokemoana 3

What is most curious about Tokemoana is his installation to the Tu'i Ha'a 'Uluakimata, which was a new line of kings, and the changes that led to the ascension and coup by Taufa'ahau against the Tu'i Tonga.

Tokemoana 2, the older son had a Samoan mother and resided mostly in Samoa. The younger brother, who resided in Tonga, was also installed to the title Tokemoana 3. The older brother, for the sake of distinction, was called Tokemoana'iHa'amoa or Tokemoana in Samoa. Tokemoana 3 had a large family of about 15 children which seem to be the trend of that time. Most chiefs and kings took on a large number of wives.

'Uluakimata 1 for example had 3 principal wives and 200 surrogate wives.

The oldest of Tokemoana 3s children was Toutaitokotaha who became Tokemoana 4. Tokemoana 4 is probably the most influential of his time and in later times through his children.

The children[10] were;
1. Tonga Toutai (Tokemoana 5)
2. Sisitoutai
3. Vaka'ulihavili
4. Teuki'utavava'u
5. Tulikitakaunove
6. Funa'ofolaha

In William Mariner's account[21], he talked about three brothers 1. Tokemoana 2. 'Ulukalala II 3. Tupouto'a who shared the same mother 'Ulukilupetea.

William Mariner was a boy of about 17 that 'Ulukalala II saved from being killed in the raid of the Port-au-Prince in 1806 and raised as his son 'Toki Ukamea' or Iron Axe.

Tokemoana in William Mariner's story was most likely Tonga Toutai or Tokemoana 5 eldest son of Tokemoana 4. It was clear from William Mariner's account that Tokemoana was the paramount chief residing at Filohivalu.

It was also clear from many accounts of the rise of Taufa'ahau, son of Tupouto'a, that it was Tokemoana who had influenced the move of the Tu'i Tonga, Laufilitonga, from Tongatapu to Lifuka, Ha'apai residing at the fort Velata. The idea being the opposition of Taufa'ahau and his group and bring them under the control of the Tu'i Tonga.

One story suggest that the war started after a challenge by Laufilitonga who summoned Taufa'ahau to Velata and admonished him for 'looking at his wife Lupepau'u while she was having a bath at the beach'. Laufilitonga suggested that Taufa'ahau is not far off from being punished to which Taufa'ahau replied, 'If you want a war, you shall have it'.

Both sides accumulated weapons and warriors before the first battle which Taufa'ahau lost[1]. History does not say why Laufilitonga let Taufa'ahau off and not kill him after he lost. It maybe Taufa'ahau escaped and persuaded a lot of other chiefs, Samoans and Fijians to join him. He even got guns and cannons from Puakatau in 'Eua.

In the second battle, Taufa'ahau was victorious and it is also curious why Laufilitonga was not killed. There is a suggestion that even though Taufa'ahau and his side won the battle they did not win the war. The office of the Tu'i Tonga was sacred and untouchable. Laufilitonga was formally installed to the Tu'i Tonga title in the next year,1827, some records suggest that it was a mockery of the Tu'i Tonga. I propose that it was the frustration of Taufa'ahau's supporters that gossip about the Tu'i Tonga installation because Taufa'ahau was still an inferior chief from an inferior line. Tupouto'a, who was Tu'i Ha'apai was not regarded very highly by the chiefs of Tongatapu who supported the Tu'i Tonga even though Tupouto'a succeeded Tupoumalohi to the title Tu'i Kanokupolu his father Tuku'aho was the 14th Tu'i Kanokupolu[1].

After the second battle of Velata, Taufa'ahau seized all of Laufilitonga's estates and possessions and even his wife, Salote Lupepau'u![30] He went on to become a Christian in 1831 and took on the name King George of Tonga becoming the head of the British Methodist Church in Tonga, who were becoming a very powerful ally. He took over the title of Tu'i Vava'u from 'Ulukalala III (1833), his first cousin who ceded to him, and also the Tu'i Kanokupolu upon Tupou's (Aleamotu'a) death in1845. Taufa'ahau even started a Parliament in 1862.

It is even more interesting that since the assassination of Taufa'ahau's grandfather Tuku'aho, the 14th Tu'i Kanokupolu (1799), by none other than the half brother of 'Ulukalala II, Tupouniua, the civil war that followed was a struggle for power and leadership of the country. It is now becoming clear that Tupoumoheofo TK12 may have ordered the assassination while she was in Vava'u[30] having being humiliated by Tuku'aho when he took the Tu'i Kanokupolu title off her and installed his own father Mumui as king. Tupoumoheofo being of higher rank in the extended family was within her authority to do so. The fact that she was never called to account for that decision is proof that all her relatives and even her enemies accepted that she was of higher rank than Tuku'aho[17].

The raid on the Port au Prince was just a part of the struggle, to obtain guns and cannons for the war which 'Ulukalala II led til his death in 1810. His younger brother Tupouto'a kept on the struggle and got himself installed to the Tu'i Kanokupolu in 1812. The fact that William Mariner mentioned 'Ulukalala II and Tupouto'a going to Filohivalu to visit Tokemoana suggest that they were simply following directions from their older brother. What is even more mind boggling is that the guns and cannons that 'Ulukalala II had might have gotten into the hands of Laufilitonga and his supporters at Velata giving them the edge

in the first battle against Taufa'ahau and his group. Of course, it was Tokemoana who brought Laufilitonga to Lifuka!
It does raise some questions as to why Laufilitonga was brought to Lifuka by Tokemoana. What was the real reason behind it? Could it be to remove him from his power base in Tongatapu then conquer him? The fact that Tongatapu was never fully brought under control until 1853 suggest that can be a motive because the chiefs of Tongatapu did not recognise Tupouto'a or even Taufa'ahau! Was that the main reason for letting Laufilitonga live? To use him as collateral against the extended family and chiefs of Tongatapu?

Tupouto'a died in 1820 which is why his son, Taufa'ahau became Tu'i Ha'apai. It is very likely that Taufa'ahau had a power struggle against his uncle Tokemoana V, who was the paramount chief of Ha'apai, older brother of his father Tupouto'a. I suggest it was the reason why Tokemoana brought Laufilitonga to Ha'apai.

There is no record of Tokemoana 5, apart from the mention in William Mariner's account, or even any children or wives. It is suspected that Tokemoana 5 died at the battle of Velata, probably the second one.

I propose that Tokemoana 5 was already very old by the time of the battle of Velata. Teuki'utavava'u, one of his younger brothers was born in 1772 so Tokemoana 5 (Tonga Toutai) is probably 6 years older so he would have been 60 years old which is like 80 or 90 years old in this day and age. The name Tongoleleka, his village in Lifuka, is legendary in the Tokemoana story because it arose from his love of the oil made from the mangrove in his old age.

There is a story that Taufa'ahau (King George Tupou I), when he chose his 33 Nobles in the first government of 1875, opposed the revival of the Tokemoana title suggesting that any Tokemoana title would be superior to his and cause conflict with his new Kingdom. Like the Tu'i Tonga title the only way to beat it, is to abolish the office of the Tu'i Ha'a 'Uluakimata and what it represents.

It is not lost on many Tongans that the choice of the name King George of Tonga was a deliberate move to bring the Methodists and British Empire on Taufa'ahau's side. Laufilitonga, on the other hand, chose to become a Catholic which was supported by the French Empire.

Tokemoana 5 may have died of old age as suggested by the story of Tongoleleka. Any children he may have had might have died in the civil war (1799-1853) in many of the battles especially the battle of Velata.

His younger brother Teuki'utavava'u also lived long. Queen Salote Tupou III[29] in one of her diaries mentioned that when the chiefs had the meeting to organize the new government, presumably of 1862, Liufau (Tu'i Ha'angana) send his son Toluta'u to summon Siotame Havea, second son of Teuki'utavava'u, to the meeting of the chiefs. Siotame thanked Toluta'u and asked him to convey his sincere gratitude to Liufau but he cannot come to the meeting as he is looking after his father Teuki'utavava'u who was very old at the time. In 1862, Teuki'utavava'u would have been 90 years old[17].

An underlying note of that message was, the family were supporting the Methodist church and were not in favour of the old kingly system. Was that why Tokemoana was never installed again? Because the family chose Jesus Christ instead of worldly titles? There is a story that many of the ancient chiefs converted to Christianity and refused titles offered by Taufa'ahau[17].

It is also noted that Teuki'utavava'u's oldest son Malakai Tonga had a daughter Ma'ata Hokulaukau'anga who married Siosifa Motu'apuaka and is one of the current Motu'apuaka's ancestors. Motu'apuaka is the 'apa'apa (talking chief directing the ceremony, Lauaki is the other on the left) on the King's right side of the famous Taumafa Kava or King's Kava Circle. He is the chief of the estate and village of Te'ekiu[17].

The Havea family is well known in the Free Wesleyan Church since Rev Sione Havea, son of Siotame Havea[10], was the Head Tutor of Tupou College in 1909. Other famous Havea names include Rev Dr Sione 'Amanaki Havea, son of Rev Sione Havea[10], former President of the FWC, Tonga, and Rev Dr Tevita Koloa'ia Havea, current Secretary of the FWC, Tonga[17]. There is also another famous Havea in Tonga, Kaveinga Havea who was a former Director of Education[17]. His son Siotame Drew Havea is another famous Havea currently based at the Pacific Islands Forum[31].

Tokemoana 5s younger brother Sisitoutai also had a large family. Some of his present day descendants include almost all of the Tongan royals and lord's families. Lord Tuita and Lord Tu'ivakano to mention two[10].

Another younger brother Vaka'ulihavili married a daughter of Tuku'ahoTK14, Finauholonga, and is one of Queen Salote Tupou IIIs ancestors through her mother

Queen Lavinia. Lord Veikune is another descendant of this brother[10].

The story of Tupoumoheofo[17]

Tupoumoheofo is very unique in Tongan history being the only female to be installed as Tu'i Kanokupolu. She was the daughter of Tupoulahimu'a, 7th Tu'i Kanokupolu. She was the 4th Moheofo, principal wife of the 36th Tu'i Tonga, Pau[10].

From all accounts Tupoumoheofo was a very political and ambitious woman. She was a princess, in her own right, but also principal wife of the paramount chief of the country[30].

From the accounts of Vason[22], who resided in Tonga for 4 years as an LMS Missionary, he was the guest of the 11th Tu'i Kanokupolu Mulikiha'amea. It seems that Tupoumoheofo who's father was the 7th king thought it would be a good idea for her to grab the Tu'i Kanokupolu title and for her son Fuanunu'iava the Tu'i Tonga title while Pau was still alive but it was Ma'ulupekotofa, Pau's older brother who succeeded and Fuanunu'iava did not become king until after Ma'ulupekotofa[17]. It seems that Muluikiha'amea was probably in favor of Tupoumoheofo to become TK12, they are first cousins, and took on the TH16[30,1] job.

The consequence of Tupoumoheofo's political ambitions was to attract the wrath of Tuku'aho who challenged Tupoumoheofo for the title of Tu'i Kanokupolu[1]. This is a very interesting development because it was generally reagarded as 'shameful' if close relatives fight and in this instance Tupoumoheofo and Tuku'aho were first cousins[17]. Tupoumoheofo's father Tupoulahi, the 7th TK, is the older brother of Mumui, Tuku'aho's father, who later became TK13. Because Tupoulahi is the elder brother Tupoumoheofo would be of higher rank than Tuku'aho. Tupoumoheofo's mother Fuonuku was the daughter of the Tu'i Ha'a 'Uluakimata, Tokemoana I, and she is the grandaughter of the 32nd Tu'i Tonga. Tupoumoheofo's mother is of higher rank than Tuku'aho's mother, a daughter of Chief Ata of Hihifo.

The fight between Tupoumoheofo and Tuku'aho was so fierce that on one island it was said the beach was covered with the bones of the dead which were left to rot with no one to bury them[17]. Eventually Tuku'aho won and Tupoumoheofo fled and took refuge at 'Ulukalala IIs residence in Vava'u. 'Ulukalala's mother 'Ulukilupetea is also a first cousin of Tupoumoheofo. Her father Ngalumotutulu is the eldest son of Ma'afu 'o Tu'i Tonga, TK6, who is also the father of Tupoulahi TK7 and Mumui TK13[10].

The events of that take over fermented some resentment of Tuku'aho's methods. Although he was hailed as a great warrior, he was also regarded as a very cruel person[1] when punishing his own supporters. The die was set because the chiefs started discussing the issue and it was decided that Tuku'aho was wrong.

Fristly, he is a lower ranked person in the family, secondly he challenged

Tupoumoheofo who was an 'annointed' king (Tu'i Kanokupolu) and he also divided the family into two factions during the ensuing war. Tuku'aho was the Governor of 'Eua when he challenged Tupoumoheofo.

Mulikiha'amea who was the 11th Tu'i Kanokupolu and probably abdicated in favor of Tupoumoheofo when he became TH16, agreed with 'Ulukalala II and his brother Tupouniua[1] to assassinate Tuku'aho, who was already the TK14 at the time, in 1799.

The assassination of Tuku'aho is the most talked about in Tongan history as it was the most probable cause of the 50 year civil war as the chiefs took sides and fought against each other. It might have been an extension of the war between Tupoumoheofo and Tuku'aho[17].

Taufa'ahau, a grandson of Tuku'aho, was only 2 years old when Tuku'aho was killed and the conflict began. He took up the fight later when his father died in 1820,

and with the help of the British
Methodists won the war and the crown[17].

Figure 1. Lists of Tu'i Tonga

Catholic List

1. 'Aho'eitu (950 AD)
2. Lolofakangalo
3. Fanga'one'one
4. Lihau
6. Kaloa
7. Ma'uhau
8. 'Apuanea
9. 'Afulunga
10. Momo
11. Tu'itatui
12. Talatama
13. Tu'itonganiu Koe Tamatou
14. Talaiha'apepe
15. Talakaifaiki
16. Talafapite
17. Tu'itonga Ma'akatoa
18. Tu'itonga Puipui
19. Havea I
20. Tatafu'ukimeimu'a
21. Lomi'aetupu'a
22. Havea II
23. Takalaua
24. Kau'ulufonua Fekai
25. Vakafuhu
26. Puipuifahi
27. Kau'ulufonua II
28. Tapu'osi II / Kau'ulufonua
29. 'Uluakimata I (Tele'a)
30. Fatafehi
31. Tapu'osi II or Kau'ulufonua II
32. 'Uluakimata I
33. Tu'ipulotu'ilangi Tu'ofefafa
34. Fakana'ana'a
35. Tu'ipulotu
36. Paulaho
37. Ma'ulupekotoafa
38. Fatafehi Fuanunuiava
39. Laufilitonga

Bakers List

1. Kohai
2. Koau
3. 'Aho'eitu
4. Lolofakangalo
5. Fanga'one'one
6. Lihau
7. Kofutu
8. Ma'uhau
9. Kaloa
10. Kaliu
11. Lingolingoa
12. Kilukilua
13. 'Apuanea
14. 'Afulunga
15. Momo
16. Lomi'aetupu'a
17. Ha'avakafuhu
18. Tu'itonga 'Ilepo
19. Puipuikifatu
20. Tu'itongapuipui
21. Kau'ulufonua Motu'a
22. Tapu'osi
23. Talakaifaiki
24. Ha'avakafuhu
25. Talafata
26. Tu'itatui
27. Talatama
28. Tu'itonga Niu Tamatou
29. Talaiha'apepe
30. Tapu'osi
31. Fatafehi
32. Havea
33. Kau'ulufonua
34. Tapu'osimonu
35. Takalaua
36. Kau'ulufonua Fekai
37. Tapu'osi
38. Tele'a
39. Fatafehi
40. Kau'ulufonua
41. 'Uluakimata
42. Tu'ipulotu
43. Fakana'ana'a
44. Tu'ipulotu'ilangi Tu'oteau
45. Pau
46. Ma'ulupekotofa
47. Fuanuinuiava
48. Laufilitonga

T.H. Fale 's List

1. 'Aho'eitu (450 AD)
2. Lolofakangalo
3. Fanga'one'one
4. Lihau
5. Kofutu
6. Ma'uhau
7. Kaloa/Kalau
8. Kaliu
9. Lingolingoa
10. Kilukilua
11. 'Apuanea
12. 'Afulunga
13. Momo I
14. Lomi'aetupu'a I
15. Ha'avakafuhu I
16. 'Ilepo
17. Puipuikifatu I
18. Puipui
19. Kau'ulufonua I
20. Tapu'osi I
21. Talakaifaiki I
22. Ha'avakafuhu II
23. Momo II/Talafata
24. Tu'itatui
25. Talatama
26. Niu Tamatou
27. Talaiha'apepe
28. Talakaifaiki II
29. Tapu'osi II
30. Fatafehi I
31. Havea I
32. Tatafu'eikimeimu'a
33. Talakaifaiki III/Lomi'aetupu'a II
34. Talafapite
35. Ma'akatoa
36. Kau'ulufonua II
37. Tapu'osi III/Havea II
38. Takalaua
39. Kau'ulufonua III (Fekai)
40. Ha'avakafuhu III
41. Puipuikifatu II / Momo III
42. Kau'ulufonua IV
43. Tapu'osi IV
44. Tele'a I /'Uluakimata I
45. Fatafehi II
46. Kau'ulufonua V
47. Tele'a II/ 'Uluakimata II
48. Tu'ipulotu'ilangi Tu'ofefafa
49. Fakana'ana'a

Cont.' Fale's List

50. Tu'ipulotu'ilangi Tu'ote
51. Paulahau / Pau
52. Ma'ulupekotofa
53. Fatafehi Fuanunuiava
54. Laufilitonga

Abbreviations.

1. TT - Tu'i Tonga
2. TH - Tu'i Ha'a Takalaua
3. TK - Tu'i Kanokupolu
4. MTH1 - First Moheofo from Tu'i Ha'a Takalaua
5. MTH2 - Second Moheofo from Tu'i Ha'a Takalaua
6. MTH3 - Third Moheofo from Tu'i Ha'a Takalaua
7. MTH4 - Fourth Moheofo from Tu'i Ha'a Takalaua
8. MTK1 - First Moheofo from Tu'i Kanokupolu
9. MTK2 - Second Moheofo from Tu'i Kanokupolu
10. MTK3 - Third Moheofo from Tu'i Kanokupolu
11. MTK4 - Fourth Moheofo from Tu'i Kanokupolu
12. MTK5 - Fifth Moheofo from Tu'i Kanokupolu
13. MTK6 - Sixth Moheofo from Tu'i Kanokupolu
14. TTF1 - First Tu'i Tonga Fefine (Female Tu'i Tonga)
15. TTF2 - Second Tu'i Tonga Fefine
16. TTF3 - Third Tu'i Tonga Fefine
17. TTF4 - Fourth Tu'i Tonga Fefine
18. TTF5 - Fifth Tu'i Tonga Fefine
19. TTF6 - Sixth Tu'i Tonga Fefine

20. TTF7 - Seventh Tu'i Tonga Fefine
21. TTF8 - Eighth Tu'i Tonga Fefine

References Cited

1. Wikipedia, the online encyclopedia

2. Menzies, G; '1421, the year China discovered the world', online sources.

3. Thor Heyerdahl, writings, theories and stories online

4. You Tube

5. Christian Bible

6. Pone, S (2020), The Moriori Evidence, Rainbow Enterprises Books, 62 p amazon.com

7. www.familysearch.org/wiki/Tonga History

8. www.facebook.com/takimamata pasifiki

9. Super Pacific City - The Lomipeau Speculation, Norman Ning Wei, www.modos.ac.nz

10. Malotonga.com/hohoko Tuputupu Le Fanua by James Cocker.

Note; much of the reference material from this source were obtained from the genealogy book by Fohe Ma'afutakinima (1903) as acknowledge by the author, James Cocker.

11. https://www.captaincooksociety.com/home/detail/a-cook-s-tour-of-tonga

12. Biography of Mary Lawry

Note; the author of this book and other details cannot be obtained as the book was on loan to the author some years ago and the source cannot be found.

13. 'Ilaiu, S.L., MSc Thesis (2007), Auckland University.

14. THE TONGAN TRADITIONAL HISTORY TALA-E-FONUA. A VERNACULAR ECOLOGY-CENTRED HISTORICO-CULTURAL CONCEPT by 'Okusitino Mahina, PhD Thesis, ANU

15. The story of Matamua

https://www.facebook.com/346003915492
277/posts/dna-to-rock-a-nationchanging-
our-new-zealand-historytears-run-from-
her-transluce/670397729719559/

16. Wordnik

17. Author's opinion, experience and
acquired knowledge

18. Tevita Fale, Tongan Astronomer
interview with Laumanu Petelo
(https://www.youtube.com/watch?v=XnU
jit5hOlM&ab_channel=TongaBroadcastin
gCommission)

19. Matangi Tonga Online Thursday 25,
February, 2021

20. https://www.jstor.org/stable/20707289?
seq=1

21. Martin J, An account of the natives of
the Tonga Islands, in the south pacific
ocean. with an original grammar and
vocabulary of their language. Compiled
and arranged from the extensive

communication of Mr William Mariner, several years resident in those islands, 1817, online sources.

Author has read this book many years ago.

22. Vason G, An authentic of narrative of four years residence at one of the Friendly Islands, 1810, online sources.

23. Capt James Cooks online records

24. The Story of Talafaiva by Semisi Pone, this publication, p 101.

25. The Story of Sinaitakala'ilangileka by Semisi Pone, this publication, p 104.

26. https://www.facebook.com/260439014 707/posts/the-tongan-calendar-was-based-on-the-phases-of-the-moon-and-had-13-months-the-ma/10151478402199708/

27. Tu'i Ha'a Takalaua Commentary by Semisi Pone, unpublished

28. Tu'i Kanokupolu Commentary by Semisi Pone, unpublished

29. Koe Tohi Hohoko 'a e Tu'i Ha'angana, online genealogy of the Tu'i Ha'angana

30. 'Ilaiu, S. L., (2019). Paradigm Shifts in Ancient Kingship Traditions in Tonga. PhD Thesis, University of Auckland. 334p.

31. https://www.forumsec.org/2018/05/11/ siotame-drew-havea-representing-civil-society-on-the-specialist-sub-committee-on-regionalism/

About the author

Semisi Pule also known as Semisi Pule Pone grew up in the Kingdom of Tonga where he learned a lot of the legends and stories of Tongan history.

After graduating from Tonga High School in 1979 he attended Mt Albert Grammar School in New Zealand in 1980 and University of Auckland in 1981, graduating with a Bachelor of Science in May, 1985.

He joined the Ministry of Agriculture, Fisheries and Forests Research Division in Tonga as a Plant Pathologist/Agriculture Officer in June, 1985. He continued his studies in 1987, also at Auckland University, and graduated with a Master of Science (Honours) in 1989. His work with MAFF, Tonga is published in his book PLANT PROTECTION IN THE PACIFIC (amazon.com)

In March 1992, he joined the University of the South Pacific (USP) Tissue Culture Project at Alafua Campus, Apia, Samoa. This project was funded by the European Union and implemented by the Institute for Research, Extension and Training in Agriculture (IRETA). His work at USP is published in his book PLANT PROTECTION IN THE PACIFIC 3, Tissue Culture (amazon.com).

In May 1993, he joined the South Pacific Commission (SPC) (now known as the Secretariat for the Pacific Community) in Suva, Fiji. He was the Plant Protection Advisor and Co-ordinator for the SPC Plant Protection Service with 7 major projects and a budget of more than $30 million. He was also responsible for the establishment of the Pacific Plant Protection Organization (PPPO) in October, 1994 and was the first Chief Executive of the PPPO from October, 1994 to April, 1996. His work at SPC is published in his books 1. PLANT PROTECTION IN THE PACIFIC, 2. CONFESSIONS OF A PATHOLOGIST AND SENIOR PLANT VIROLOGIST, 3.

DOUG WATERHOUSE, a great Australian (amazon.com) and also in several advisory ebooks (amazon.com).

Due to some health problems he moved with his family to Auckland, New Zealand where he was involved in various industries. He began writing in 2010 and has published more than 300 books in amazon.com, blurb.com and wheelers.co.nz to date.

He is also passionate about gardening and music and has developed some watermelon hybrids as well as new ukulele tunes.

More information about his other activities can be viewed in his website www.thefamouswriter.co.nz

www.ingramcontent.com/pod-product-compliance
Lightning Source LLC
La Vergne TN
LVHW051349080426
835509LV00020BA/3349